LIVE TO MAKE
A DIFFERENCE

LIVE TO MAKE A DIFFERENCE

An Inspiring Call to Action

Max Lucado

THOMAS NELSON
Since 1798

NASHVILLE   DALLAS   MEXICO CITY   RIO DE JANEIRO

Published in Nashville, Tennessee, by Thomas Nelson. Thomas Nelson is a registered trademark of Thomas Nelson, Inc.

Thomas Nelson, Inc. titles may be purchased in bulk for educational, business, fund-raising, or sales promotional use. For information, please e-mail SpecialMarkets@ThomasNelson.com.

All of the text in this booklet is taken from *Outlive Your Life* © 2010 Max Lucado.

Unless otherwise noted, Scripture quotations are taken from the New King James Version®. © 1982 by Thomas Nelson, Inc. Used by permission. All rights reserved.

Scripture quotations marked ESV are from the English Standard Version. © 2001 by Crossway Bibles, a division of Good News Publishers.

Scripture quotations marked MSG are from *The Message* by Eugene H. Peterson. © 1993, 1994, 1995, 1996, 2000, 2001, 2002. Used by permission of NavPress Publishing Group.

Scripture quotations marked NCV are from the New Century Version®. © 2005 by Thomas Nelson, Inc. Used by permission. All rights reserved.

Scripture quotations marked NLT are from the Holy Bible, New Living Translation. © 1996, 2004. Used by permission of Tyndale House Publishers, Inc., Wheaton, Illinois 60189. All rights reserved.

Any italics in the Scripture quotations reflect the author's own emphasis.

ISBN 978-0-8499-4612-7

Printed in the United States of America

10 11 12 13 14 QG 5 4 3 2 1

CONTENTS

Dear Friend,

May I take just a moment to introduce you to a story that is very dear to my heart?

It's a story of hillbillies and simple folk, net casters and tax collectors. A story of a movement exploded like a just-opened fire hydrant out of Jerusalem and spilled into the ends of the earth: into the streets of Paris, the districts of Rome, and the ports of Athens, Istanbul, Shanghai, and Buenos Aires. A story so mighty, controversial, and head spinning that two millennia later a middle-aged, redheaded author from Texas would be writing a book that wonders:

Might it happen again?

Walking through the first twelve chapters of Acts, we see firsthand how a few faithful people can change the world. And we're asking, *Lord, do it again.*

May God use us to make a difference.

— Max

It's Called Life

By the time you knew what to call it, you were neck deep in it. It's called life. And this one is yours.

No one else has your version. You'll never bump into yourself on the sidewalk. You'll never meet anyone who has your exact blend of lineage, loves, and longings. Your life will never be lived by anyone else.

Life is racing by, and if we aren't careful, you and I will look up, and our shot at it will have passed us by.

But if you're anything like me, it's not enough for you to do well. You want to do good. You want your life to matter. You want to live in such a way that the world will be glad you did.

But how can you? How can I? Can God use us?

I have one hundred and twenty answers to that question. One hundred and twenty residents of ancient Israel. They were the charter members of the Jerusalem church (Acts 1:15). Fishermen, some. Revenue reps, others. A former streetwalker and a converted revolutionary or two. They had no clout with Caesar, no friends at the temple headquarters. Truth be told, they had nothing more than this: a fire in the belly to change the world.

The book of Acts announces, "God is afoot!"

Is he still? we wonder. *Would God do with us what he did with his first followers?*

Heaven knows we hope so. One billion people are hungry,[1] millions are trafficked in slavery, and pandemic diseases are gouging entire nations. Each year nearly 2 million children are exploited in the global commercial sex trade.[2] Every five minutes, almost ninety children died of preventable diseases.[3] More than half of all Africans do not have access to modern health facilities. And as a result, 10 million of them die each year from diarrhea, acute respiratory illness, malaria, and measles. Many of those deaths could be prevented by one shot.[4]

Yet in the midst of the wreckage, here we

stand—the modern-day version of the Jerusalem church. You, me, and our one-of-a-kind lifetimes and once-in-history opportunity.

A mere 2 percent of the world's grain harvest would be enough, if shared, to erase the problems of hunger and malnutrition around the world.[5] There is enough food on the planet to offer every person twenty-five hundred calories of sustenance a day.[6] We have enough food to feed the hungry.

I don't mean to oversimplify terribly complicated issues. We can't just snap our fingers and expect the grain to flow across borders. Policies stalemate the best of efforts. International relations are strained. Corrupt officials snag the systems. I get that.

But this much is clear: the storehouse is stocked. The problem is not in the supply; the problem is in the distribution. God has given this generation, *our generation*, everything we need to alter the course of human suffering.

We are given a choice . . . an opportunity to make a big difference during a difficult time. What if we rocked the world with hope? Infiltrated all corners with God's love and life? What if we followed the example of the Jerusalem church?

"We are God's masterpiece. He has created us anew in Christ Jesus, so we can do the good things he planned for us long ago" (Eph. 2:10 NLT). We are created by a great God to do great works. He invites us to outlive our lives, not just in heaven but here on earth.

Live with Passion

CHAPTER 1

The Nazareth Manifesto

Jesus, in his first message, declared his passion for the poor. Early in his ministry he returned to his hometown of Nazareth to deliver an inaugural address of sorts. He entered the same synagogue where he had worshipped as a young man and looked into the faces of the villagers. They were simple folk: stonecutters, carpenters, and craftsmen. They survived on minimal wages and lived beneath the shadow of Roman oppression. There wasn't much good news in Nazareth.

But this day was special. Jesus was in town. The hometown boy who had made the big time. They asked him to read Scripture, and he accepted. "And He was handed the book of the prophet Isaiah. And when He had opened the book, He found the place where it was written . . ." (Luke 4:17).

This is the only such moment in all the Gospels. Jesus *quoted* Scripture many times. But the Son of God, selecting and reading Scripture? This is it. On the singular occasion we know of, which verse did he choose? He shuffled the scroll toward the end of the text and read, "The Spirit of the LORD is upon Me, because He has anointed Me to preach the gospel to the poor; He has sent Me to heal the brokenhearted" (Luke 4:18, quoting Isaiah 61:1).

Jesus lifted his eyes from the parchment and quoted the rest of the words. The crowd, who cherished the words as much as he did, mouthed the lines along with him: "To proclaim liberty to the captives and recovery of sight to the blind, to set at liberty those who are oppressed; to proclaim the acceptable year of the LORD" (Luke 4:18–19).

"This is my mission statement," Jesus declared. The Nazareth Manifesto.

❖

Dadhi is an Ethiopian farmer, a sturdy but struggling husband and father. His dirt-floored mud hut would fit easily in my garage. His wife's handwoven baskets decorate his walls. Straw mats are rolled and stored against the sides, awaiting nightfall when all seven family members will sleep on them.

Dadhi earns less than a dollar a day at a nearby farm. He'd work his own land, except a plague took the life of his ox. His only one. With no ox, he can't plow. With no plowed field, he can't sow a crop. If he can't sow a crop, he can't harvest one.

All he needs is an ox.

Dadhi and I share the same aspirations and dreams. We have much in common. Then why the disparity? Why does it take Dadhi a year to earn what I can spend on a sport coat?

Part of the complex answer is this: he was born in the wrong place. He is, as Bono said, "an accident of latitude."[1] A latitude void of unemployment insurance, disability payments, college grants, Social Security, and government supplements. A latitude largely vacant of libraries, vaccinations, clean water, and paved roads. I benefited from each of those. Dadhi has none of them.

You don't have to travel sixteen hours in a plane to find a Dadhi or two. They live in the convalescent home you pass on the way to work, gather at the unemployment office on the corner. They are the poor, the brokenhearted, the captives, and the blind.

No one can do everything, but everyone can do something. Some people can fast and pray about social sin. Others can study and speak out. What about you? Why not teach an inner-city Bible study? Use your vacation to build houses in hurricane-ravaged towns? Run for public office? Help a farmer get an ox?

Speaking of which, I received a note from Dadhi the other day. It included a photo of him and a new family member. A new three-hundred-pound, four-legged family member. Both of them were smiling. I'm thinking God was too.

CHAPTER 2

Our Small Part, God's Big Part

It is hard to look suffering in the face. Wouldn't we rather turn away? Stare in a different direction? Fix our gaze on fairer objects? Human hurt is not easy on the eyes.

What do we see when we see . . .

- the figures beneath the overpass, encircling the fire in a fifty-five–gallon drum?
- the news clips of children in refugee camps?
- reports of 1.75 billion people who live on less than $1.25 a day?[1]

What do we see? "When [Jesus] saw the multitudes, He was moved with compassion for them, because they were weary and scattered, like sheep having no shepherd" (Matt. 9:36).

This word *compassion* is one of the oddest in Scripture. The New Testament Greek lexicon says this word means "to be moved as to one's bowels . . . (for the bowels were thought to be the seat of love and pity)."[2] It shares a root system with *splanchnology*, the study of the visceral parts. Compassion then is a movement deep within—a kick in the gut.

Perhaps that is why we turn away. Who can bear such an emotion?

A couple in our congregation lives with the heart-breaking reality that their son is homeless. He ran away when he was seventeen, and with the exception of a few calls from prison and one visit, his parents have had no contact with him for twenty years. His mom allowed me to interview her at a leadership gathering. As we prepared for the discussion, I asked her why she was willing to disclose her story.

"I want to change the way people see the homeless. I want them to stop seeing problems and begin seeing mothers' sons."

Change begins with a genuine look. And continues with a helping hand. I'm writing this chapter by a dim light in an Ethiopian hotel only a few miles and hours removed from the home of Bzuneh Tulema.

Bzuneh lives in a two-room, dirt-floored, cinder-block house at the end of a dirt road in the dry hills of Adama. Maybe three hundred square feet. He's painted the walls a pastel blue and hung two pictures of Jesus.

Across from me, Bzuneh beams. He wears a Nike cap with a crooked bill, a red jacket (in spite of furnace-level heat), and a gap-toothed smile. No king was ever prouder of a castle than he is of his four walls. As the thirty-five-year-old relates his story, I understand.

Just two years ago he was the town drunk. He drank away his first marriage and came within a prayer of doing the same with the second. He and his wife were so consumed with alcohol that they farmed out their kids to neighbors and resigned themselves to a drunken demise.

But then someone *saw* them. Members of an area church took a good look at their situation. They began bringing the couple food and clothing. They invited them to attend worship services. Bzuneh was not interested. However, his wife, Bililie, was. She began to sober up and consider the story of

Christ. The promise of a new life. The offer of a second chance. She believed.

Bzuneh was not so quick. He kept drinking until one night a year later he fell so hard he knocked a dent in his face that remains to this day. Friends found him in a gully and took him to the same church and shared the same Jesus with him. He hasn't touched a drop since.

It all began with an honest look and a helping hand. Could this be God's strategy for human hurt? First, kind eyes meet desperate ones. Next, strong hands help weak ones. Then, the miracle of God. We do our small part, he does the big part.

I will make you as a light for the nations,
that my salvation may reach to the end
of the earth.

—*Isaiah 49:6* ESV

❋

O Lord, what an amazing opportunity you
have spread out before me—a chance to
make a difference for you in a desperately
hurting world. Help me to see the needs you
want me to see, to react in a way that honors
you, and to bless others by serving them
gladly with practical expressions of your love.

Live with Purity

CHAPTER 3

Self-Serving or Serving Others?

When Jesus saw a religious hypocrite, he flipped on the spotlight and exposed every self-righteous mole and pimple. "They love to pray standing in the synagogues and on the corners of the streets, that they may be seen by men" (Matt. 6:5).

The Greek word for hypocrite, *hupokrites*, originally meant "actor." First-century actors wore masks. A hypocrite, then, is one who puts on a mask, a false face.

Jesus did not say, "Do not do good works." Nor did he instruct, "Do not let your works be seen."

We must do good works, and some works, such as benevolence or teaching, must be seen in order to have an impact. So let's be clear. To do a good thing is a good thing. *To do good to be seen* is not. In fact, to do good to be seen is a serious offense. Here's why.

Hypocrisy turns people away from God. When God-hungry souls walk into a congregation of wannabe superstars, what happens? When God seekers see singers strut like Las Vegas entertainers . . . when they hear the preacher—a man of slick words, dress, and hair—play to the crowd and exclude God . . . when other attendees dress to be seen and make much to-do over their gifts and offerings . . . when people enter a church to see God yet can't see God because of the church, don't think for a second that God doesn't react. "Be especially careful when you are trying to be good so that you don't make a performance out of it. It might be good theater, but the God who made you won't be applauding" (Matt. 6:1 MSG).

Hypocrisy turns people against God. So God has a no-tolerance policy. Let's take hypocrisy as seriously as God does. How can we?

1. *Expect no credit for good deeds.* None. If no one notices, you aren't disappointed. If someone does, you give the credit to God. Ask yourself this question: "If no one

knew of the good I do, would I still do it?" If not, you're doing it to be seen by people.

2. *Give financial gifts in secret.* Money stirs the phony within us. We like to be seen earning it. And we like to be seen giving it. So "when you give to someone in need, don't let your left hand know what your right hand is doing" (Matt. 6:3 NLT).

3. *Don't fake spirituality.* When you go to church, don't select a seat just to be seen or sing just to be heard. If you raise your hands in worship, raise holy ones, not showy ones. When you talk, don't doctor your vocabulary with trendy religious terms. Nothing nauseates more than a fake "Praise the Lord" or a shallow "Hallelujah" or an insincere "Glory be to God."

Bottom line: don't make a theater production out of your faith. "Watch me! Watch me!" is a call used on the playground, not in God's kingdom. Silence the trumpets. Cancel the parade. Enough with the name-dropping. If accolades come, politely deflect them before you believe them. Slay the desire to be noticed. Stir the desire to serve God.

Focus on the inside, and the outside will take care of itself. Lay your motives before God daily, hourly. "Search me, O God, and know my heart; test me and know my anxious thoughts. Point out anything in me that offends you, and lead me along the path of everlasting life" (Ps. 139:23–24 NLT).

Do good things. Just don't do them to be noticed.

CHAPTER 4

Let the Walls Tumble Down

Do any walls bisect your world? There you stand on one side. And on the other? The person you've learned to disregard, perhaps even disdain. The teen with the tats. The boss with the bucks. The immigrant with the hard-to-understand accent. The person on the opposite side of your political fence. The beggar who sits outside your church every week.

Or the Samaritans outside Jerusalem.

Talk about a wall, ancient and tall. "Jews," as John wrote in his gospel, "refuse to have anything to do with Samaritans" (John 4:9 NLT). The two cultures had hated each other for a thousand years. The feud involved claims of defection, intermarriage, and disloyalty to the temple. Samaritans were black-listed. Their beds, utensils—even their spittle—were considered unclean.[1] No orthodox Jew would travel into the region. Most Jews would gladly double the length of their trips rather than go through Samaria.

Jesus, however, played by a different set of rules. He spent the better part of a day on the turf of a Samaritan woman, drinking water from her ladle, discussing her questions (John 4:1–26). He stepped across the cultural taboo as if it were a sleeping dog in the doorway. Jesus loves to break down walls.

How does God feel about the person on the other side of your wall?

> He tore down the wall we used to keep each other at a distance . . . Instead of continuing with two groups of people separated by centuries of animosity and suspicion, he created a new kind of human being, a fresh start for everybody.
>
> Christ brought us together through his death on the cross. The Cross got us to embrace, and that was the end of the hostility. (Eph. 2:14–16 MSG)

The cross of Christ creates a new people, a people unhindered by skin color or family feud. A new citizenry, based not on common ancestry or geography but on a common Savior.

My friend Buckner Fanning experienced this firsthand. He was a marine in World War II, stationed in Nagasaki three weeks after the dropping of the atomic bomb. Can you imagine a young American soldier amid the rubble and wreckage of the demolished city? Radiation-burned victims wandering the streets. Atomic fallout showering on the city. Survivors shuffling through the streets, searching for family, food, and hope. The conquering soldier, feeling not victory but grief for the suffering around him.

Instead of anger and revenge, Buckner found an oasis of grace. While patrolling the narrow streets, he came upon a sign that bore an English phrase: Methodist Church. He noted the location and resolved to return the next Sunday morning.

When he did, he entered a partially collapsed structure. Windows, shattered. Walls, buckled. The young marine stepped through the rubble, unsure how he would be received. Fifteen or so Japanese were setting up chairs and removing debris. When the uniformed American entered their midst, they stopped and turned.

He knew only one word in Japanese. He heard

it. *Brother*. "They welcomed me as a friend," Buckner relates, the power of the moment still resonating more than sixty years after the events. They offered him a seat. He opened his Bible and, not understanding the sermon, sat and observed. During communion the worshippers brought him the elements. In that quiet moment the enmity of their nations and the hurt of the war was set aside as one Christian served another the body and blood of Christ.

Another wall came a-tumblin' down.

We can't live to make a difference if we can't get beyond our biases. Who are your Samaritans? Whom have you been taught to distrust and avoid?

It's time to remove a few bricks.

Therefore, accept each other
just as Christ has accepted you
so that God will be given glory.

—Romans 15:7 NLT

Lord, in how many ways does my foolish
heart make false distinctions among your
people? Reveal them to me. Rebuke me in
your love. Lend me divine insight, and bless
me with the resolve to be your hands and feet.

Live with Power

CHAPTER 5

Powerful Things Happen When We Pray

King Herod suffered from a Hitler-level obsession with popularity. He murdered the apostle James to curry favor with the populace. The execution bumped his approval rating, so he jailed Peter and resolved to behead him on the anniversary of Jesus' death.

He placed the apostle under the watchful eye of sixteen Navy Seal sorts. They bound him in chains and secured him three doors deep into the prison.

Peter in prison is just the first of a long list of challenges too big for the church.

So our Jerusalem ancestors left us a strategy.

When the problem is bigger than we are—we pray! "But while Peter was in prison, the church prayed very earnestly for him" (Acts 12:5 NLT).

One of our Brazilian church leaders taught me something about earnest prayer. We knelt on the concrete floor of our small church auditorium and began to talk to God. Change that. I talked; he cried, wailed, begged, cajoled, and pleaded. He pounded his fists on the floor, shook a fist toward heaven, confessed, and reconfessed every sin. He recited every promise in the Bible as if God needed a reminder.

Most of us struggle with prayer. We forget to pray, and when we remember, we hurry through prayers with hollow words. Our minds drift; our thoughts scatter like a covey of quail. Why is this? Prayer requires minimal effort. No location is prescribed. No particular clothing is required. No title or office is stipulated. Yet you'd think we were wrestling a greased pig.

Speaking of pigs, Satan seeks to interrupt our prayers. He knows the stories; he witnessed the angel in Peter's cell and the revival in Jerusalem. The devil knows what happens when we pray. "Our weapons have power from God that can destroy the enemy's strong places" (2 Cor. 10:4 NCV).

Satan tries to position himself between us and God. But he scampers like a spooked dog when we move forward. So let's do.

> Humble yourselves before God. Resist the devil, and he will flee from you. Come close to God, and God will come close to you. (James 4:7–8 NLT)

In late 1964 Communist Simba rebels besieged the town of Bunia in Zaire. A pastor by the name of Zebedayo Idu was one of their victims. They sentenced him to death before a firing squad and placed him in jail for the night. The next morning he and a large number of prisoners were herded onto a truck and driven to a public place for execution. With no explanation the official told the prisoners to line up and number off—"one, two, one, two, one, two." The ones were placed in front of the firing squad. The twos were taken back to the prison. Pastor Zebedayo was among those who were spared.

Back in the jail cell, the prisoners could hear the sound of gunfire. The minister took advantage of the dramatic moment to share the story of Jesus and the hope of heaven. Eight of the prisoners gave their lives to God that day. About the time Pastor

Idu finished sharing, an excited messenger came to the door with a release order. The pastor had been arrested by mistake and was free to leave.

He said good-bye to the prisoners and hurried to his home next to the chapel. There he discovered a crowd of believers urgently praying for his release. When they saw the answer to their prayers walk through the door, their prayer service became a praise service.[1]

The same God who heard the prayers from Jerusalem heard the prayers from Zaire. He is still listening. Are we still praying?

CHAPTER 6

God Uses Common Folk

Does Jesus still use simple folks like us to change the world? We suffer from such ordinariness. The fellow to my right snoozes with his mouth open. The gray-haired woman next to him wears earphones and bobs her head from side to side. They don't wear halos or wings. They don't emit any light.

Most of us don't. We are common folk. We sit in the bleachers, eat at diners, change diapers, and wear our favorite team's ball cap. Chauffeurs don't drive our cars; butlers don't open our doors or draw our baths. We, like the Jerusalem disciples, are regular folk.

Does God use the common Joe?

Edith would say yes.

Edith Hayes was a spry eighty-year-old with thinning white hair, a wiry five-foot frame, and an unquenchable compassion for South Florida's cancer patients. I was fresh out of seminary in 1979 and sitting in an office of unpacked books when she walked in and introduced herself: "My name is Edith, and I help cancer patients." She extended her hand. I offered a chair. She politely declined. "Too busy. You'll see my team here at the church building every Tuesday morning. You're welcome to come, but if you come, we'll put you to work."

Her team, I came to learn, included a hundred or so silver-haired women who occupied themselves with the unglamorous concern of sore seepage. They made cancer wounds their mission, stitching together truckloads of disposable pads each Tuesday, then delivering them to patients throughout the week.

Edith rented an alley apartment, lived on her late husband's pension, and ducked applause like artillery fire.

The battalion led by Joe and Liz Page has a different objective—doll-sized wardrobes for premature infants. They turn one of our church classrooms into a factory of volunteer seamstresses. Joe and Liz make sure these children have something to wear, even if they wear it to their own funerals.

Joe retired from military service. Liz once taught school. He has heart problems. She has foot deformities. But both have a fire in their hearts for the neediest of children.

As does Caleb. He's nine years old. He plays basketball, avoids girls, and wants the kids of El Salvador to have clean drinking water.

He took the twenty dollars he had been saving for a new video game, gave it to the cause, and asked his father to match it. He then challenged the entire staff of the children's ministry at his church to follow his example. The result? Enough money to dig two wells in El Salvador.

Edith, Joe, Liz, and Caleb are regular folks. They don't have a seat at the United Nations or a solution for the suffering in Darfur. But they do embrace this conviction: God doesn't call the qualified. He qualifies the called.

Don't let Satan convince you otherwise. He will try. He will tell you that God has an IQ requirement or an entry fee. That he employs only specialists and experts, governments and high-powered personalities. When Satan whispers such lies, dismiss him with this truth: God stampeded the first-century society with swaybacks, not thoroughbreds. Before Jesus came along, the disciples were loading trucks, coaching soccer, and selling Slurpee drinks at the convenience store. Their collars were blue, and their hands were calloused, and there is no evidence that Jesus chose them because they were smarter or nicer than the guy next door. The one thing they had going for them was a willingness to take a step when Jesus said, "Follow me."

I was hungry, and you fed me. I was thirsty, and you gave me a drink. I was a stranger, and you invited me into your home. I was naked, and you gave me clothing. I was sick, and you cared for me. I was in prison, and you visited me.

—Matthew 25:35–36 NLT

❀

O Lord, where did I see you yesterday . . . and didn't recognize you? Where will I encounter you today . . . and fail to identify you? O my Father, give me eyes to see, a heart to respond, and hands and feet to serve you wherever you encounter me!

CONCLUSION

When We Love Them, We Love Him

There are many reasons to help people in need. But for the Christian, none is higher than this: when we love those in need, we are loving Jesus. It is a mystery beyond science, a truth beyond statistics. But it is a message that Jesus made crystal clear: when we love them, we love him.

Jesus will recount, one by one, all the acts of kindness. Every deed done to improve the lot of another person. Even the small ones. In fact, they all seem small. Giving water. Offering food. Sharing clothing. The works of mercy are simple deeds. And yet in these simple deeds, we serve

Jesus. Astounding, this truth: we serve Christ by serving needy people.

The Jerusalem church understood this. How else can we explain their explosion across the world? What began on Pentecost with the 120 disciples spilled into every corner of the world. Antioch. Corinth. Ephesus. Rome. The book of Acts, unlike other New Testament books, has no conclusion. That's because the work has not been finished.

Many years ago I heard a woman discuss this work. She visited a Catholic church in downtown Miami, Florida, in 1979. The small sanctuary overflowed with people. I was surprised. The event wasn't publicized. I happened to hear of the noon-hour presentation through a friend. I was living only a few blocks from the church. I showed up a few minutes early in hopes of a front-row seat. I should have arrived two hours early. People packed every pew and aisle. Some sat in windowsills. I found a spot against the back wall and waited. I don't know if the air-conditioning was broken or nonexistent, but the windows were open, and the south coast air was stuffy. The audience was chatty and restless. Yet when she entered the room, all stirring stopped.

No music. No long introduction. No fanfare

from any public officials. No entourage. Just three, maybe four, younger versions of herself, the local priest, and her.

The father issued a brief word of welcome and told a joke about placing a milk crate behind the lectern so we could see his guest. He wasn't kidding. He positioned it, and she stepped up, and those blue eyes looked out at us. What a face. Vertical lines chiseled around her mouth. Her nose, larger than most women would prefer. Thin lips, as if drawn with a pencil, and a smile naked of pretense.

She wore her characteristic white Indian sari with a blue border that represented the Missionaries of Charity, the order she had founded in 1949. Her sixty-nine years had bent her already small frame. But there was nothing small about Mother Teresa's presence.

"Give me your unborn children," she offered. (Opening words or just the ones I remember most? I don't know.) "Don't abort them. If you cannot raise them, I will. They are precious to God."

Who would have ever pegged this slight Albanian woman as a change agent? Born in a cauldron of ethnic strife, the Balkans. Shy and introverted as a child. Of fragile health. One of three children. Daughter of a generous but unremarkable businessman. Yet somewhere along her journey, she became convinced that Jesus walked in the "distressing disguise of the poor," and she set out to love him by loving them. In 1989 she told a reporter that her Missionaries had picked up around fifty-four thousand people from the streets of Calcutta and that twenty-three thousand or so had died in their care.[1]

I wonder if God creates people like Mother Teresa so he can prove his point: "See, you can do something today that will outlive your life."

How You Can
Make a Difference

Let's follow the example of the Jerusalem church. Let's live out the twenty-ninth chapter of the book of Acts. Let's write the story of the church for our generation!

MY ACTION PLAN
TO ROCK OUR WORLD WITH HOPE

1. Pray first: I will commit to pray daily about these needs and my own participation in alleviating suffering:

_____

_____

_____

_____

_____

_____

_____

_____

2. Put my commonness in God's hands: I will offer my gifts and how God might use them in service to others in:

* **My home and church**

_____

_____

_____

_____

_____

* **My community**

_____

_____

_____

_____

_____

* My world

_____

_____

_____

_____

_____

_____

3. Live to make a difference: here's how my
   small part, God's big part will have a
   permanent place on my calendar:

_____

_____

_____

_____

_____

For more ideas on how you can be a difference-maker, read *Outlive Your Life: You Were Made to Make a Difference*. Included inside, you will discover additional information, suggestions, and inspiration.

Remember, you can't do everything, but everyone can do something.

Notes

Introduction: It's Called Life

1. Food and Agriculture Organization of the United Nations, *The State of Food Insecurity in the World: Economic Crises—Impacts and Lessons Learned*, 2, ftp://ftp.fao.org/docrep/fao/012/i0876e/i0876e.pdf.

2. UNICEF, *The State of the World's Children 2007: Women and Children; The Double Dividend of Gender Equality*, 5, www.unicef.org/sowc07/docs/sowc07.pdf.

3. That equals approximately 25,000 per day. Anup Shah, "Today, Over 25,000 Children Died Around the World," *Global Issues*, www.globalissues.org/article/715/today-over-25000-children-died-around-the-world.

4. Peter Greer and Phil Smith, *The Poor Will Be Glad: Joining the Revolution to Lift the World out of Poverty* (Grand Rapids: Zondervan, 2009), 26.

5. Ronald J. Sider, *Rich Christians in an Age of Hunger: Moving from Affluence to Generosity* (Nashville: Thomas Nelson, 2005), 10.

6. Ibid., 35.

Chapter One: The Nazareth Manifesto

 1. "Closer to the Music," U2.com, 30 July 2003, www
    .u2.com/news/article/682.

Chapter Two: Our Small Part, God's Big Part

 1. UNICEF, *The State of the World's Children 2009:
    Maternal and Newborn Health*, www.unicef.org/
    sowc09/report/report.php.
 2. James Strong, *New Strong's Exhaustive Concordance*
    (Nashville: Thomas Nelson, 1996), s.v. "Compassion."

Chapter Four: Let the Walls Tumble Down

 1. Hilary Le Cornu with Joseph Shulam, *A Commentary
    on the Jewish Roots of Acts* (Jerusalem: Netivyah Bible
    Instruction Ministry, 2003), 403.

Chapter Five: Powerful Things Happen When We Pray

 1. R. Kent Hughes, ed., *Acts: The Church Afire*
    (Wheaton, IL: Crossway Books, 1996), 169–70.

Conclusion: When We Love Them, We Love Him

 1. David Aikman, *Great Souls: Six Who Changed the
    Century* (Nashville: Word Publishing, 1998),
    199–221, 224.

You could be the answer to a child's prayer. When you sponsor a child, you will be providing things like food, shelter, clothing, clean water, education, and hope for a brighter future.

Help Change
a **Life**

9780849920691, $24.99

Are you ready now to explore the larger message of *Outlive Your Life*?

You'll discover:

- what is your Jerusalem, Judea and Samaria, and ends of the earth
- how God still uses simple folks to change the world
- why now is the time to act on a once-in-history opportunity

WWW.MAXLUCADO.COM

THOMAS NELSON
Since 1798

thomasnelson.com

978-1-4185-4394-5
$34.99

978-1-4185-4395-2
$9.99

Dig in with Max Lucado through four DVD sessions that follow real-life stories of people who are making their lives count. Designed for individual study or a small group experience, the *Outlive Your Life* study shows you how to make everything in your life—your time, your skills, your passions—add up to something bigger than you.

THOMAS NELSON
Since 1798

thomasnelson.com

978-1-4003-1649-6
$16.99

978-1-4041-8783-2
$15.99

978-1-4003-1600-7
$14.99

Now that you've discovered the incredible message of *Outlive Your Life*, share it with your friends, kids, and teens.